Nature's Window

PENGUINS

Nature's Window

PENGUINS

Sheila Buff

ANDREWS AND MCMEEL
A UNIVERSAL PRESS SYNDICATE COMPANY
KANSAS CITY

INTRODUCTION

Penguins are the oddest and most endearing of birds. Comically awkward on land yet gracefully agile underwater, these large, flightless birds are superbly adapted to life at sea. They thrive in the iciest waters and coldest temperatures on earth. Although they are also found in the Southern Hemisphere, as far north as New Zealand, the Falkland Islands, and

King Penguins breed in colonies that may contain hundreds of thousands of birds. The colonies are on level, ice-free beaches on cold, windswept, rocky islands scattered in the South Atlantic Ocean.

even the Galápagos Islands near the equator, penguins have come to symbolize the cold antarctic region at the bottom of the globe.

In the seventeenth century, European seafarers sailing the cold seas and exploring the rugged coasts of the Southern Hemisphere were baffled by the first penguins they encountered. What was this creature that walked upright on two legs like a human, swam underwater like a fish, had flippers like a seal, and laid eggs like a bird? Even the dense feathers of a penguin are unlike those of almost any other bird: very stiff and short, they overlap tightly above a thick layer of down. Except for their inability to fly, however, the penguins strongly resembled auks, a type of Northern Hemisphere bird already familiar to the European explorers, so they concluded correctly that the penguins were birds as well.

THE PENGUIN FAMILY

Although all penguins share the same basic coloration, black or dark gray feathers on their upper body parts and white below, they differ mainly in size and in the coloring and ornamentation of their heads. Of the seventeen or eighteen members of the penguin family (experts differ on exactly how many species there are), the largest and per-haps best known is the Emperor Penguin. This elegant, robust bird stands up to four feet tall, weighs as much as eighty-five pounds, and has

The Emperor Penguin is the largest member of the penguin family. Shown here with two downy chicks, Emperor penguins breed on the inhospitable Antarctic continent, the coldest place on earth.

flippers that are more than a foot long. Emperor Penguins live in colonies that can include up to 350,000 members. They breed on the coast and ice floes of Antarctica, the coldest, driest, and windiest continent on earth, where winter temperatures hover around forty degrees Fahrenheit below zero.

The next biggest penguin, the King Penguin, stands around three feet tall and weighs about thirty pounds. King Penguins can be found just below the Antarctic Circle on frigid, windswept, rocky islands scattered in the South

Atlantic Ocean, including such barren spots as Kerguelen Island, Macquarie Island, and South Georgia Island.

At the other extreme, the smallest member of the penguin family, the Little Penguin of New Zealand, once called a Fairy Penguin until its aggressive nature was discovered, weighs only a bit more than two pounds and stands a little over a foot tall. Unlike any other penguins, the Little Penguin, also called the Blue Penguin, has no bright colors or ornamentation on its head. Instead, its upper parts are a uniform bluish-gray or blue-black color.

The Yellow-eyed Penguin, while not the smallest in size, has the smallest population of any penguin. Found only in southeastern New Zealand and a few islands off the coast, this species has a population of only about thirty-five to forty-five hundred birds, and is endangered.

Three related penguin species have shorter, stiffer tails than other penguins, live in crowds of thousands on the Antarctic pack ice or nearby, and are all about the same size. They include the Gentoo, Adélie, and Chinstrap Penguins.

The King Penguin, the second-largest penguin, stands about three feet high and weighs twenty-five to thirty pounds. It is found on Antarctica and on the barren islands of the subantarctic region.

Uncommon penguins

The crested penguin family, consisting of six related species, is distinguished by unusual head feathers. All the birds of this family have ornamental crests of yellow or orange plumes that project outward behind their red or red-brown eyes, rather like vividly colored, very spiky eyebrows. The six species include the Rockhopper Penguin, the Fiordland Penguin, the Snares Penguin (which breeds only on Snares Island off the coast of New Zealand), the Erect-crested

The spiky, yellow-gold plumes, the bright red eyes, the massive bill, and the wonderfully oversized webbed feet of the Macaroni Penguin give it a distinctively rakish appearance.

Penguin, the Macaroni Penguin, and the Royal Penguin. Macaroni Penguins breed in huge colonies. More than eleven million breeding pairs can be found on the Antarctic continent and on nearby islands.

Although we usually think of penguins as cold-weather birds, four uncommon species of penguins live in warm climates. The most northerly penguin, the Galápagos Penguin, breeds on desert islands almost directly on the equator. The African Penguin (also sometimes called the Jackass

The Little Penguin, also called the Blue Penguin, is the smallest of the penguin family. Unlike any other penguin, the Little Penguin has no colors or ornamentation on its head.

Penguin) is found only on the southernmost coast of South Africa; the Magellanic Penguin is found on the southern tip of South America and on the Falkland Islands. The Humboldt Penguin relies on the Humboldt Current—which flows along the coasts of Chile and Peru—for food. Except for the Magellanic Penguin, which has a population of anywhere from one to two million, warm weather penguins are far less numerous. Together, there are about ten thousand Humboldt and Galápagos Penguins, for example.

A Falkland Islands Magellanic Penguin has a beak full of nesting material. Both male and female birds help build the nest, lining it with grasses, twigs, and feathers.

Because they forage for fish in the frigid waters of the Antarctic region and breed on the pack ice that covers the continent in the winter, most Emperor Penguins walk only on ice and never on land. During the perpetual twilight of the long Antarctic winter, they trudge for miles across the pack ice to reach their breeding colonies inland.

Locomotion on land

The characteristic image of a penguin is of a waddling, slightly comical bird. But although penguins on land may seem clumsy, they can move with surprising dexterity. Penguins' legs are quite short and are set far back on their bodies, which gives them their upright stance and waddling gait. They walk erect most of the time, sometimes covering long distances. While many species travel a mile inland to nest, Emperor Penguins may walk over the Antarctic pack ice for more

It's easy to see how the Rockhopper Penguin gets its name. To reach the ocean, this small penguin jumps, hops, and bounces down the steep slopes of the rocky islands and then jumps feetfirst into the water.

than 120 miles to reach their inland nesting sites.

Penguins also run, with their flippers extended back behind them for balance, and waddle, hop, or jump from place to place. Penguins can generally leap the length of their bodies, but before jumping across a crevice in the ice, they lean over and peer across to judge the distance.

Rockhopper Penguins, as their name suggests, almost always hop with their feet together to climb up the rocky shores and cliffs of their environment. When they are heading downhill

Chinstrap Penguins are quite agile, using both feet and flippers to maneuver over uneven terrain. They can jump across gaps over three feet wide, several inches more than their height.

toward the ocean, they hop, jump, and even slide, falling often, and then jump feetfirst into the water.

When penguins really want to move fast on snow or ice, they toboggan on their bellies, pushing themselves along with their flippers and braking with their feet. Tobogganing downhill is faster than walking or hopping. Emperor Penguins can toboggan for hundreds of miles along the ice. Amazingly, penguins can toboggan uphill in some areas by pulling themselves up with their flippers and then sliding along.

Penguins have very short legs and waddle awkwardly on land. Those that live in colder regions, such as these Emperor Penguins in the Antarctic, often toboggan on their bellies to move quickly over ice and snow.

Swimming and Diving

Unlike most other birds, penguins don't fly. Instead, they swim through the ocean waters much as most other birds fly through the air. Seemingly slow and awkward on land, in the sea penguins are speedy and graceful as they search for fish, squid, and krill (tiny, shrimplike creatures that teem in the cold waters of the Antarctic region).

Chinstrap Penguins wade into the ocean off the Antarctic coast in search of their favorite food, krill. Although all penguins breed on land, many of them spend as much as 80 percent of their time at sea.

Penguins enter the water either from shore or through a hole or crack in the ice. To get farther out into open water, penguins swim

with flipper strokes or make shallow dives. When penguins pursue a school of fish or other prey or try to evade a predator such as a sea lion, they "porpoise" by making shallow dives, coming up briefly for air, and diving again. Penguins porpoise faster than they swim, reaching speeds of four to five miles per hour when porpoising.

Penguins dive underwater to capture their prey. They use their powerful flippers for propulsion and steer with their webbed feet and tails. Their waterproof feathers, heavy down insulation, and thick layer of body fat help them survive the icy, cold water of the Antarctic.

Penguins can dive to amazing depths and stay down for minutes at a time. Most dive three hundred feet or less, but in the deepest dive ever recorded by researchers, an Emperor Penguin dove over thirteen hundred feet.

The larger the penguin, the longer it can stay submerged. Small penguins usually stay underwater for about a minute, medium-sized penguins for three to six minutes, and larger ones for about eight minutes. One unusual Emperor Penguin had a dive that lasted eighteen

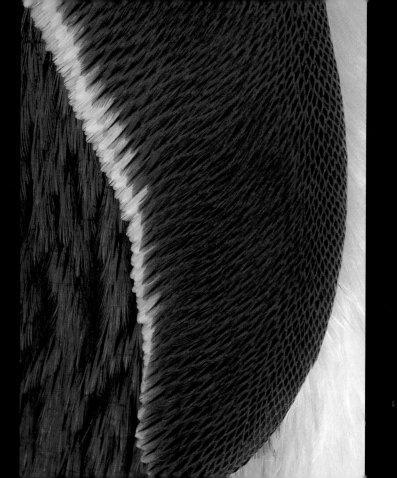

minutes. Scientists still don't understand how penguins stay submerged for so long without breathing or how they withstand the changes in water pressure as they dive.

When returning to shore after feeding, penguins porpoise as the water gets shallower and then bodysurf or jump onto shore. Predators such as sea lions and leopard seals often lurk in the murky water near shore, hoping to catch a penguin as it returns. If the penguins see a predator, however, they confuse it by leaping straight up out of the water in a starburst pattern.

Penguins have very short, stiff, lance-shaped feathers packed densely all over their bodies. Overlapped tightly on top of a layer of insulating down, the feathers provide effective insulation against the cold.

BREEDING BEHAVIOR

Penguins breed in large, noisy, smelly colonies—colonies of Adélie Penguins may contain half a million birds. In these crowded settings, male penguins use some form of ecstatic display as a way to attract the notice of a female. The male starts out by beating his flippers slowly and rhythmically while arching his neck and thrusting out his chest. He then stretches his whole body up and points his bill at the sky, beating his flippers. The display is accompanied by a loud braying

A mated pair of Gentoo Penguins bow toward each other and then throw back their heads and make a harsh braying or trumpeting noise, a display performed to reinforce their bond as a breeding pair.

or trumpeting call. Once a male attracts a mate, they form a monogamous bond that endures for years. To reinforce this bond they continue to use different types of display behavior similar to the mating behavior.

To make their nests, most penguins make a scoop or hollow in the ground and line it with coarse grass, pebbles, shells, or sometimes bones. Since these items are scarce on the treeless, barren nesting grounds, each pair must jealously protect its own nest while attempting to steal building materials

These Chinstrap Penguins incubate their eggs by lying over them. The nests, built of stones, feathers, and bones, are evenly spaced about two feet apart. Parent birds share the job of incubation.

from neighbors. The nests in a penguin colony are generally spaced just out of pecking range from one another. A few penguin species, such as the Little Penguin, make nesting burrows under the ground.

Female penguins of most species generally lay two eggs a few days apart. During the incubation period (from thirty to sixty days, depending on the species), the parent birds usually take turns sitting on the eggs. In some species, such as the Rockhopper Penguin, one parent's shift can be ten to twelve

Emperor Penguin chicks huddle together in a crèche for warmth and protection. Parent birds and chicks recognize each other's voices. When a parent calls, a chick will respond with a squeal.

days long, while the other parent is off feeding in the ocean. During this time, the parent bird stays on the nest continually and does not feed. In some species, this fasting period is quite long. Male Adélie Penguins fast for some thirty-five days, while both male and female Macaroni Penguins fast for as long as forty days.

After the chicks hatch, the parent birds brood them for the next two weeks to keep them warm and protect them from predatory birds such as gulls and petrels. Once the chicks grow larger, however, they huddle together in crèches while their parents go off for one to three days to feed in the open ocean. Parent birds feed the chicks by regurgitating food into the chicks' mouths. In many species, the chick chases after the parent begging for food, just as do almost all other baby birds.

In one of the most unusual breeding strategies in the bird world, male Emperor and King Penguins are responsible for incubating their eggs. The males hold the eggs on top of their feet and cover them with a special fold of skin; chicks are brooded (kept warm and protected) in the same way. Incubation takes place in the depth of the dark, frigid Antarctic winter. For the entire nine-week incubation period, while the female penguins disperse out to sea to hunt for food, the male penguins huddle together without eating. Shortly after the eggs hatch, the female penguins return, find their mates and newborn chicks, and take over the brooding duties. The males, having fasted

An Emperor Penguin chick peers out from under its parent's protective abdominal fold, where it will stay for several weeks, until it is large enough to huddle with other chicks when its parents go to feed.

all this time, finally return to the ocean to hunt for food. They soon come back, however, to help the females care for the chicks.

DANGERS TO PENGUINS

Penguins in general are long-lived birds, often surviving for fifteen years. Predators are a constant danger, however. Sea lions, killer whales, sharks, and leopard seals prey on penguins at sea. On land, adult penguins have no real predators, but they do have some unnatural ones. Because penguin territory is so desolate, most penguins are fearless in the presence of people. Although penguins taste terrible, whale hunters once slaughtered them in large

Seals and sea lions are the major threats to penguins. In this unusual instance, a leopard seal hauls itself onto an ice floe in pursuit of Adélie Penguins. More often, they lurk in shallow water and wait to attack.

numbers for the meat and boiled them for oil. By the early 1900s, the King Penguin population on Macquarie Island was nearly exterminated in this way. When the killing was banned, the population quickly recovered. On some islands and coastal breeding areas, introduced animals such as cats, pigs, foxes, and rats prey on eggs and chicks, while cattle sometimes trample nests.

Today almost all penguin populations are quite large, numbering in the hundreds of thousands or even millions. Most of these populations are healthy, but some face threats from oil spills, overfishing, and habitat loss at breeding sites. As humans encroach more on the pristine waters in search of fish and oil, havens such as specially protected areas may be needed.

Penguins enchant us with their antics and charm us by their social behavior—they are very popular exhibits at zoos and aquariums. Fortunately, the world's penguins are surviving and even thriving in their distant homes, as well. Our growing worldwide awareness of environmental protection will help keep them safe forever.

Photography credits

All images provided by Ellis Nature Photography
©Gerry Ellis: pages 4, 13, 14, 17, 19, 20-21, 22, 29, 32, 34, 37
©Konrad Wothe: pages 2, 9, 25, 26, 39, 43, 44
Front jacket: ©Konrad Wothe
Back jacket: ©Gerry Ellis

ISBN: 0-8362-2784-0

Printed in Hong Kong

First U.S. edition
1   3   5   7   9   10   8   6   4   2

Editor: Linda Hetzer
Art director: Susi Oberhelman
Designer: Yolanda Monteza

Produced by Smallwood and Stewart, Inc., New York City